JOURNEY
TO
SUCCESS

JOURNEY TO SUCCESS

FRED J. FELTON

ARPress

ILLUMINATING IDEAS.
EMPOWERING VOICES

ARPress
45 Dan Road Suite 5
Canton MA 02021

Hotline: 1(888) 821-0229
Fax: 1(508) 545-7580

Ordering Information:
Quantity sales. Special discounts are available on quantity purchases by corporations, associations, and others. For details, contact the publisher at the address above.

Printed in the United States of America.

ISBN-13:	Softcover	979-8-89389-768-5
	eBook	979-8-89389-769-2

Library of Congress Control Number: 2024923274

Journey to Success is dedicated to everyone determined to succeed in spite of adversity. It serves as a "road map" that will guide you through life's challenges. It is especially dedicated to my family.

Review of Journey to Success by Fred J Felton

Journey to Success by Fred J. Felton is an inspiring and thoughtful exploration of one young man's determination to overcome the obstacles of growing up on the south side of Chicago. Felton dives deep into the challenges of inner-city life, illustrating how relationships, health, sex, spirituality, and moral responsibility play critical roles in shaping our success.

The book is more than just a personal story; it's a guide that examines the consequences of the choices we make and how those decisions shape our future. Felton provides readers with a candid look at the realities of life in a tough neighborhood while offering insights into the values and mindset needed to persevere. The combination of personal reflection and practical advice makes Journey to Success both engaging and educational.

Felton's narrative touches on universal themes, making this a must-read for anyone interested in personal growth, resilience, and the pursuit of success despite adversity. With its powerful message and relatable journey, Journey to Success is an uplifting read for those looking to reflect on their own paths and choices.

★★★★★ 5.0 out of 5 stars "Journey to Success" - Trials, Tribulation, and Triumph...

Reviewed in the United States on August 29, 2010

Peace, Love, & Harmony to All...

If you've experienced trials & tribulations in life and you aren't sure how to overcome this is the book for you. Fred utilizes his life's journey through the storm to assist you, get through yours. He takes an extremely traumatic situation at the age of 14 and reflects by connecting to spirituality to rise above and move forward... Instead of giving up from then to now he now contributes to the world. "Journey to Success" is an inspirational book, it's a must have to carry with you through life...

Fred, took this moment in life to actually embrace life, some might have taken it in the complete opposite direction. But, Fred took a negative situation as a time to improve his path in life, readjust which isn't always easy to do. Especially, with this type of scenario Fred experienced. When life is out of balance, what becomes the answer? We must reevaluate our life and make a change, that's exactly what Fred did...

We all know that times are interesting and challenging with the global economy and conditions of life. But, let's view life in general as the `glass being half full, and not half empty. Opportunities, for your visions and a better tomorrow do exist. Let's pierce through the eye of the storm, and you'll see them there... Let's appreciate that which we have, the successes in our lives and let "Journey to Success" allow it to be one of those choices to get things started in your life...

TABLE OF CONTENTS

Poems by Fred J.

Introduction

The clear and deep blue sky was lit up with planets and stars. In my mind, I reached out and touched each star and traveled the universe from planet to planet. The universe was inside me and the galaxy was a welcome relief from the jungle of Chicago's south side that I lived in. This night was unusually dark and the dry, hot air was suffocating. It was August and unbearably humid tonight. Dad walked up to me while I was in the backyard contemplating and gazing towards the sky. It was 2 am, dad's shadow kind of scared me.

"Fred J, what are you doing?" he said. "I am trying to figure out how the sky, stars, moon, planets and wind came to be and if my life is worth living." My dad was always willing to talk to me about anything. He looked at me and said, "God created everything in the universe! You know a man could not have done it. Do you know any man who could create a universe"? I didn't know any such person, so I accepted dad's explanation. But why was I here? More specifically, who am I and what is this life really all about? Up until this moment I had never thought about my life or what mattered to me the most. I had just dropped out of high school at fifteen years old and didn't have a clue about what I was going to do with the rest of my life.

Dad is 6'2, and stayed in good shape even though he didn't work out that much, if at all. He worked all day as a furniture repairman and drove cabs evenings and weekends to make ends meet. Dad spent the rest of his time at church, where he was a deacon or working in the garage or around the house. He and mom were always there for me, but I did things my way. I was a fifteen-year- old black man, living on the south side of Chicago amidst the gangs, poverty and violence with a dream to succeed. During this period of my life, I felt like I was in a world with no hope, and I really didn't want to be bothered by anyone. My life was swallowing me up and I had so many things on my mind.

Our home is a nice little frame house on the corner with a front and side yard, and a fairly large backyard equipped with a flower / vegetable garden and patio. Dad was always grooming the yard and chasing the squirrels away from his green tomatoes. We also had a berry tree that supplied mom with all the switches she ever needed to tan Julia, Brian and my backsides.

All of my family loved to hang out in the backyard and watch the neighbors walk by the side of the house. When my friends and I would hang out on the side of the house fraternizing, sometimes the police would make us disburse or go inside the yard. They once frisked me and a couple of my friends and threatened to arrest us for standing on the side of "my own" house.

My brother Brian was born twelve months and twelve days before me. He has always been a little leaner and slightly taller than me. My sister Julia is about three years older than me. Both my siblings were always very smart and were always there to advise me. Julia won the eighth-grade science fair and later received a college scholarship and Brian has always been extremely talented in music. Brian actually could play any instrument he wanted to. He first played guitar, then later decided to become a piano player.

We have always been a close-knit family with strong Christian values. Mom didn't tolerate any nonsense from any of us at home or at school and I was cutting classes, hanging out over at Rodney's house during the day and then playing chess every night over at Chucks. Mom didn't waste any time letting me know that I was screwing my life up. She was constantly preaching to me to straighten up and didn't understand why I wasn't applying myself in school. My eighth-grade math teacher, Mr. Riggs, told the class one day that half of all his students would be hanging on the street corner, homeless and jobless. I was beginning to think he meant me.

Earlier in the day, ten gang members had chased me and stabbed me several times while I was with Chuck and Rodney going to pick up some marijuana. Chuck was the splitting image of a young Morgan Freeman and Rodney was a tall light skinned, pretty boy with good hair. I used to spend all my free time with Chuck and Rodney. Those were my home boys, and we had each other's back. When we arrived at the weed house, Chuck stopped to let me out of the car to go and get the weed. I got out of Chuck's car and walked up to the house. As soon as I reached the front porch, I recognized some of the gang members that I had a previous altercation with. All the guys had long sharp knives and processed hair and I knew then I had better get back to the car fast.

Rodney usually carried a piece because once while he was on the west side of Chicago walking down a dark alley, two men put a gun to his back and told him to take off his $200 shoes. After Rodney was robbed that day, he always carried a piece and I was expecting to hear some shooting. I sprinted back to the car and was going to jump through the open window, but Chuck pulled off and I was left standing alone in the street, with ten guys chasing me with knives. I quickly looked back and all I could see was the sharp glare from the hot August sun reflecting from their knives in my eyes. They were running towards me pointing their steel blades, swiping viciously. I dodged the knives and ran as fast as I could to get away. There was a trash can standing at the corner of the alley and I snatched it and slung it at the guy's head that was closest to me and kept running.

Just then Chuck and Rodney came driving back and were trying to run these guys over. Chuck caught up with me, picked me up, blood was flowing from my body all over his car, and he rushed me to his house which was around the corner from mine. I am very fortunate that I wasn't killed that day, but the incident may have saved my life. Chuck later explained that he didn't mean to pull off and leave me but he just reacted when he saw all those knives flashing. While I was still in Chuck's car, I realized someone must have already told my mom that I had been stabbed because I saw a short lady running frantically down the street with her heels flying off her feet. I must have passed out then because the next thing I knew, I was getting stitched up at the hospital. Rodney told me later that an ambulance took me to the hospital from Chuck's house.

Now I was at home, trying to figure out why I, a fifteen-year-old sophomore, was in this situation with these gangsters. The gangs have caused problems as far back as I can remember. When I was ten or eleven years old, my dad took my brother and me to the neighborhood McDonald's. I went in the restaurant, purchased our food and left. As soon as I exited McDonald's, a gang member, who I did not see, was hiding at the time and appeared out of nowhere and snatched the bag of food out of my hand while running. He ran towards some guys standing on the opposite corner of the street. I went back to the car with no food and told my brother and dad what happened. My dad and brother and I drove off looking for them, but they were gone with our lunch.

We often walked or ran several blocks out of our way to reach our destinations because the gangs took our bikes and our money every time they saw us, if they could. Hopefully when you ran into the gangs, one of them would be someone you knew and they would only hit you in the chest or upside your head a few times. If not, you just had to give up your money or get beat up. Sometimes the gangs would go on recruiting missions and hang out on every corner and walk down the streets. It was difficult to go anywhere without being harassed. Every time I walked to the store the gangs were on the corner ready to take my money or hit me if I didn't have any change to give them. Some of my friends were gang members. They lived across the street, around the corner, and down the street from me. Most of my old friends that were in gangs eventually moved out of the neighborhood, went to prison or were murdered. When I was twelve years old, I was in the junior disciples by default. I never joined the gang, but I was guilty by association.

One Saturday afternoon after coming from basketball practice, myself and seven or eight guys on my church basketball team were taking the train back home. The Blackstone Rangers (street gang) got on the Englewood train, and we knew they were going to rob us. They were in leather jackets with red tams leaning to the side on their heads. My friend Ricky was wearing my new coat and I was wearing Ricky's coat. It was a new warm, white cotton coat that my mom and dad had just bought for me. In Chicago you need a warm coat! One of them liked my comfortable new white coat. The gang member told Ricky to stretch his arms out to see if the coat fit his arms. Ricky stretched his arms as ordered and the gang member said it looked like a good fit so he took my coat. At first, we only saw about five or six of them and started getting courageous and thought we were ready to fight, then, all of a sudden, about thirteen gang members came into our train from another train. They lined the whole team up and threatened to beat all of us up right there on the train. It was kind of funny because our center, Herman was the biggest and the tallest guy on the team. He was sitting next to an adult and lowered his head so the gang members wouldn't notice him. They never said a word to Herman, maybe because although he was only fourteen years old, he was over six feet tall and looked like a grown man at the time. There were at least twenty passengers riding the train but no one dared to get involved and step in to help us. The Blackstone Rangers took my coat and all the money we had and then left the train. None of the passengers on the train ever said a word. When I was fourteen and went to high school my life fell apart. It seemed like all high school was about was getting high and trying to have sex with all the girls. I was deep into rock music and learned how to drink and smoke weed. My older friends would go to the corner liquor store and pay the wine heads on the corner to buy beer, Thunderbird or Wild Irish Rose. We would walk down the alley behind our homes passing a joint, drinking beer or wine.

I loved elementary school and was rather smart but high school didn't address any of the problems that I had. There was too much time wasted on irrelevant subjects like drafting, and machine shop. I was going to be a songwriter, not a drafter or lathe operator. I didn't understand why there were so many gangs in my environment that I had to run and hide from them every day just to stay alive. Many of my neighborhood friends had been to jail and were back in the neighborhood. Guys would come back from jail and start burglarizing homes and robbing people. Crime was everywhere. You name it, auto theft, drugs, murder, rape, prostitution.

It was on the south side of Chicago during the 70's. Mom and dad bought the house that I grew up in before I was born. I grew up there and knew everybody's name in the neighborhood and everybody knew my name. We had block parties with D J's, bands and outdoor barbecues. Children, teenagers and adults hung out and played board games, cards and volleyball. Of course, Chuck, Rodney and I and the rest of my partners would have a drink and a smoke for the occasion. My friends and their moms were my extended family. I was over Chuck and Rodney's house more than I was at my own home. The neighbor who saw you everyday would let you know when you screwed up and you could be sure they would tell your mom if you did something bad. My friends and I played basketball or softball almost every day with the guys from around the block. We played "it" with the girls. In case you never played "it", let me briefly explain. Someone must volunteer to be "it", or you choose the person to be "it". Whoever is decided to be "it" must catch another person and tag them. The tagged person becomes "it" also and they continue to catch and tag the other people until everyone is caught ("it" was really fun when the girls caught you!).

On warm summer nights we would take the neighborhood girls to Rainbow Beach at Lake Michigan to chill out until curfew when the cops would run us away. But there was the bad side. The fights! You had to fight just to survive in the neighborhood. My brother, friends and I studied martial arts and stayed in shape in order to try and defend ourselves against the gangsters, thugs, wine heads, hustlers, and dope dealers that lurked on the streets all night long. In 1972, the gangs literally chased me out of high school. Math was one of my favorite subjects and I never wanted to cut math class, but one day when I arrived at class, my classmate Margaret told me that five or six guys were looking for me and one of the guys was in our class. I knew exactly who it was, and I immediately left school and ran to the bus stop. I had beaten a couple of those guys up when they approached me one on one demanding that I give them their money. I knew they were going to try to get me back. They saw me waiting at the bus stop and started running towards me. The bus wasn't coming so I started running down the street and they began chasing me. I had run about three blocks when I saw someone I knew driving home from school. I ran and caught up with the car when it stopped and banged on the hood. My friend shockingly looked at me, unlocked the door and I got in the car. I had gotten away this time but somehow, I knew I would meet up with them again. All this trouble with the gangs started in the school store one day while I was cutting my machine shop class. A couple of guys with leather jackets and processed hair approached me and told me to sell marijuana to my friends. I said no and they pulled out long sharp knives and insisted that I take a few bags of weed to sell and make a little profit. I sold some bags to my friends and we smoked a few bags up. One of my friends stole the weed money that I had already made. It was only thirty or forty dollars but I almost got killed over it.

I am very fortunate that my life did not end on the days the ten guys were chasing me with knives, trying to kill me. I was stabbed several times on my right and left arm and received about thirty stitches. It could have been worse. That incident may have saved my life because I thought about why that happened to me. Crime was everywhere and I had become a part of it. The streets were bad on the south side of Chicago.

> Take a little walk with me
> You'll be surprised at what you might see
> Take a little walk with me
> You'll be surprised, yea You'll be surprised
> At what you might see.
> Won't you take a little walk with me?
> Down in the valley
> Through the mountains and trees
> You'll see things you've never seen
> I will tell you stories that you've never heard
> All True
> Word for Word
> You'll never have to worry or fear getting lost
> I won't go towards roads that we can't cross
> Take a little walk with me
> You'll be surprised at what you might see
> Take a little walk with me
> You'll be surprised, uh huh now
> You'll be surprised, yea
> You'll be surprised, uh huh now
> At what you might see!

I had transferred to another high school but ran into a member of the same gang who recognized me. He told me that if I didn't bring him the money, they would kill me. I didn't have the money, so I took mom's meat cleaver to school instead and met him in the restroom after 3rd period. I wound up throwing it at him and quickly leaving school. The trouble with the gangs intensified over the summer. Gang members were calling me several times a day threatening to "fuck me up or kill me". They would drive by the house over and over, looking for me. I was scared for my life, so I obtained a sawed-off shotgun to protect myself. One of the guys drove by and pointed a knife at me while telling me he was going to "fuck me up". I showed him the shotgun and he drove off. I wore jeans and tennis shoes every day when I walked around the neighborhood and I always kept my shotgun strapped to my leg with my mom's garter belt. I had to always be prepared to defend my life, and I constantly stayed aware of everybody around me. I didn't know when or where I would see these gang members. After the incident at school with the butcher knife, I never went back to school. That was the second high school that the gangs had chased me out of. I just skipped school, stayed home and played my bass guitar, wrote songs and sold weed. I had no future and was going nowhere at all. I was a victim of the ghetto, dazed and confused, drowning in my sorrow. And every time mom had meat to tenderize and she couldn't find her meat cleaver, mom would look towards me then ask everybody in the kitchen "Has anybody seen my meat cleaver"? Of course, I didn't say a word. Mom and Dad never really knew that these guys seriously wanted to kill me and I never asked them for the money. If they had loaned me the money I probably wouldn't have given it to the gangsters anyway.

Mom fought with me about hanging out with my friends and prayed continuously for me. She told me to do something other than play my bass and get high all the time. My Godmother told me to go to church. My dad had faith in me when I didn't even understand what faith was. He always told me to "keep pushing". My cousin Sandra was a high school principal and she told me that if I passed the General Education Development test (GED) with a good score, she could get me enrolled in junior college. I went to night school and studied for the GED test and even though all my friends previously warned me that the test was hard and I would fail, I passed the test on the first try. I advised Sandra that I had passed the test, and she came by the house and counseled my mom and me about going to college and to help me apply for financial aid. She convinced my mom that I was actually going to go to school and obtain my degree. Mom signed the financial aid papers. Sandra then introduced me to Ms. Singleton who was over a program for minority students at Northeastern Illinois University. Ms. Singleton gave me several assessment tests and after passing the assessments I immediately enrolled in college and studied English, Music and Philosophy, like I had always wanted to.

I remember taking creative writing, basketball and tennis. College was so much more fun than high school and it was completely different. There were no gangs hanging around the schools trying to hustle me and instead of taking machine shop I could take the classes that I enjoyed. I was going to be an English teacher or a songwriter / musician not a lathe operator. I was sixteen and for the first time in my life, deep down inside, I believed in myself. I felt that if I pushed myself, I could accomplish my goals and succeed in life. But I still had to keep the shotgun strapped to my leg in the hood because the gangs were still driving around every day looking for me.

My brothers and sister have always pushed me to be the best I could be at everything. We were very competitive in everything: academics cards, chess, driving, music, or whatever. Actually, there was no comparison at all with Brian in music. My brother was and still is a musical genius. At the time, Julia had already received her Bachelor's degree and Brian was near completing his Bachelor's degree. I wanted my college degree very badly now, not just to compete with my brother and sister but because I had screwed up so had badly in high school and now, I wanted to make amends.

My play brother Ted is a year or so older than Brian. Ted is not biological, but he has always been there for my brother and me. He kind of grew up with our family. We didn't want to be in any gangs or cause trouble. We were just righteous young people that wanted to have fun and be successful in life. I was determined to get my degree and obtain a good job and move away from the ghetto and rise above the infectious diseases that have demonized me in the past. My goal was to be successful in my life as a songwriter, musician or an English teacher, but most of all I wanted to have peace of mind.

When I started college, I felt like there was some resentment from some of my "home boys". Sometimes they would tease me about how I was wasting my time trying to get an education, and I understood. All day long I was in a college classroom, learning and studying, away from the crime that lurked outside in the inner city. Then I would come home from school and hang out, drink, and get high with the home boys and expect them to have my back if the gangs drove by looking for me.

When I was nineteen years old, I met Pam. My home boys and I were playing basketball against the guys on the other side of the viaduct. She would be my next girlfriend and future wife. I saw a short, cute, athletically built girl standing at the other end of the court with her girlfriends and I called for the ball and immediately went in for a slam dunk. I was 5'10 ½" & about 145 lbs. back then and had about a 30-inch vertical leap. I dribbled in to the paint, jumped and lunged toward the basket for the dunk. An opposing player slid across the lane to block me out and I flipped over his shoulder and went flying towards the cement. My head was headed for the cement, but I somehow luckily landed on my back, breaking my fall and preventing slamming my head into the pavement. My friends told me that the ball actually went in after bouncing off the rim. I asked Pam if she saw me dunk the ball and fall to the ground. And she said "no". I was instantly attracted to her.

Pam and I lived on opposite sides of the viaduct nearly a mile apart. The Blackstone Rangers street gang ran the turf on her side of the viaduct and the Disciples street gang owned my side of the viaduct. I used to run from Pam's house to my house in less than six minutes. I ran partly for conditioning but mainly to avoid being confronted by the gangs. One evening after school I stopped in the playground to play chess with Chuck. We were in the middle of a competitive game when 3 cars filled with people pulled up in the alley at the rear of the playground. There were teenagers, adults, girls and guys with baseball bats and sticks invading the kid's playground running towards us. Chuck told me they were looking for the people who had broken up a fight earlier in the day. Chuck told me to "get up and run". I didn't want to run. I wanted to fight but after looking at those folks hollering and screaming storming towards me with bats and sticks, I decided it was best to run to the car and just drive off from the playground.

My grades were pretty good at Northeastern Illinois University but the distractions in the neighborhood were affecting my focus on school. I had a B plus average and mom told me that if I worked and saved some money, she would sacrifice some of her hard- earned money to help send me downstate to Southern Illinois University in Carbondale Ill, to complete my degree. I worked at a security job and saved some money. Mom contributed as promised and I went downstate to college. Before I left home to go to SIU in January, my relationship with Pam was starting to get serious and I didn't really want to leave her at this time, but I was on a mission, and I knew she would understand.

My brother and sister had gone to local Universities and after a month of being away at college I was thinking that I should have done the same. I had a nice little basement apartment behind the train tracks, not too far from the campus bookstore. It had large, ground level windows that wouldn't lock. If I wasn't home, Terry, a friend that I have known for years, would enter my apartment through the window and wait for me until I came in from school. I had no food in my refrigerator and was flat broke, but I did have my electric bass and contra bass and I was in the jazz band, studying with a string bass instructor in hopes of joining the University symphony orchestra.

One day, I went to my private bass lesson and I was weighing about 130 lbs. I was so thin that my string bass instructor took me to McDonald's instead of having a lesson. I was so broke that I used to sell books that I "found" lying unattended around campus to get money for food. I sold so many books back to the bookstore that eventually the store clerks wouldn't buy books from me anymore. I was on the chess team and was actually pretty good. I finished 3rd in a Midwest regional tournament held at SIU in 1977 and I would play chess for money to get so I could purchase beer and pizza. I called home once to complain about not having any money. It was winter and some pipes had just frozen and broken in the house. My mom and dad had to repair the pipes and had other bills. They could not spare any extra money. My dad told me to "Keep pushing," that "if there is a will, then there is a way". I am sure dad meant well but I really didn't want to hear that. When spring came, I tried out for the SIU Salukis baseball team just to see if I could still play the game. I was pretty good at baseball when I was a kid and as a freshman, I had made the high school baseball team but quit because some of my peers teased me about the tight uniform. The coach told me that "he saw some talent" and if I practiced with the team all summer that I could play next year. I called my dad and asked him to send me some money to buy a baseball glove. Dad sent the money, and I spent it on beer and pizza. A couple of my friends at school had bank accounts that their parents had set up for them to use, and they had cash cars to go to work or ride around in. I wanted some new clothes, some money and maybe a car. I was tired of being broke and dropped out of college at the end of the semester and moved back to my mom and dad's house. I didn't have enough will power to persist through the adversity and had quit on myself again. I was twenty years old and back in the neighborhood that I so badly wanted to get away from. It was the same thing all over again in the hood except there was more crime than before and the gangs had become more violent. I loved my family and the good friends from the neighborhood that I had grown up in. There were many good memories back home, but I hated being there amidst the drugs, gangs, prostitution, unemployment and hopeless conditions in general. It seemed like every August the murder rate on the south side of Chicago went up higher and higher. I was tired of the south side jungle of Chicago and I was determined to get out by any means necessary. In August of 1977, I went to the Air Force reserves recruiting office. The recruiter told me all kinds of good things about the reserves, and I was sold immediately. Pam would understand that I had another mission to go on. I joined the service and left without telling anyone. Mom told me later that my nephew cried when he found out I had left. I immediately felt bad for not saying goodbye to my family and friends before leaving. It's just that nobody had ever cried for me before, and I didn't think anyone would care.

I went to Lack Land, Air Force Base in San Antonio, Texas for basic training and after basic I would be leaving to Lowry, AFB in Colorado for technical school. I was going to be a procurement specialist and live and be stationed in Denver, Colorado. My uncle Curtis lived in Aurora, Colorado and worked for Braniff, Airlines. He was going to let me stay with him and then get me a job with the airline. Later I would marry Pam, and we would live happily forever after in Colorado. Basic training went well until two days before graduation. I was assigned to be the dorm guard monitor and had completed every training discipline with flying colors but then I got into a fight with a white boy in the barracks. I remember it well. It was after 9pm and I told this airman to turn his night light off and go to sleep. He pointed his finger at me and told me that "he didn't have to listen to me". He said that "his dad was the Mayor of Iowa, and I was a piece of shit and he didn't have to listen to me". Well, I was the dorm guard monitor, and he had to listen to me today. I shoved his finger back and knocked his head into the lock on his locker. His head started bleeding, and he started running and screaming to get out of the dormitory. I shouted an order to my guards not to let him out of the dorm room, but he bolted out the dorm room anyway and ran down stairs to the officer's quarters bleeding and complained to the officers. I will make a long story short. I was out of the Air Force and on my way back to the South Side of Chicago. I did get an honorable discharge after going to a jag but before you know it I was back at my mom's house and my plans to have a career in the Air Force marry Pam and live happily ever after in Denver, Colorado had fallen apart very quickly. What was this cycle? Why could I not get away from my mom's house? School didn't work, the military didn't work. What was I going to have to do to get away from the hood? Was it my destiny to be a wine head or drug addict like the guys I have grown up watching on the corner every day? Would I be unemployed like the vast majority of people in the area? Maybe I would become a victim to crime like so many black males do on a daily basis? There is a thin line between good and bad, between being in the wrong place at the wrong time. If you walk the inner-city streets three hundred sixty-five days a year, there's a good chance you will become a victim of circumstances. Many of the guys I grew up with have been to prison. Could I avoid that fate, or was it inevitable?

A couple years after I came back from the Air Force, Pam and I were married. We were both twenty-three years old and all we had was a dream and thankfully a job. We were living paycheck to paycheck, but we enjoyed life with our friends and family. Soon we had two sons, and I was chasing my dream of being a songwriter, musician and getting my college degree while trying to be a husband and father at 25 years old. It was a more difficult task than I had originally thought it would be. Pam's mom and sisters watched our boys when they were young. We didn't have enough money to pay for a day care center for infant care so if it wasn't for her family I don't know who would have watched the kids while we worked. My factory job at the printing company was stable until Reaganomics hit in the early eighties and I was laid off work. Unless I had a job interview, I would go over to my vocalist's (Pete's) house to write songs and play our original music. Pam would get tired of me hanging out with my friends writing songs, playing music and coming home late drunk, or high.

Mr. Jack, the 60-year-old man who lived across the street from my mom had taught me how to handicap the horses when I was sixteen. He used to stagger out of his door, coughing horrifically, walking slowly to grab the handrails on the stairs. He coughed so bad I thought he was dying from emphysema. He would sit on the porch and read his racing form. One day he called me over and I spoke to him. After that he taught me how to read the daily horse racing form and I would go to the racetrack with him and run his bets to the window for him. I found out soon that Mr. Jack didn't have emphysema, but he did have some very potent weed. Well, it was tough trying to take care of a family on an unemployment check so, I would take my unemployment compensation check to Belmont Park, Maywood Park or Sportsman's Park and bet on the horses to try and double my money. Sometimes I would win an extra few hundred dollars. Once or twice, I won a few thousand but most of the time I broke even or loss.

Pam and I had some good times with family and friends, but we struggled financially to survive. It was frustrating not having a permanent job, working for six to eight weeks and then getting laid off. My job would eventually call me back but by then we were further behind in our bills and had spent any money we had previously saved just to make it through my lay off. That was very taxing on my wife, family and me. In 1985, our lake front apartment was broken into by local gang members while Pam and I were asleep.

Our apartment was in a large court way and Lake Michigan was 100 feet to the left of our front door. We lived on the 3rd floor and could see miles over the Lake from our living room window. The windows were so large that you could easily jump out of them if you wanted too. There were steel fire escape steps in the back that led up to the back door that we kept burglar bars on and there was a window a couple of feet to the right of the stairs that led to the kitchen. We also had burglar bars on the front door, but we kept the key in the lock in case we needed to exit the apartment in a hurry. I came in late one night and fell sound to sleep. I felt Pam nudging me and I woke up. She pointed to our bedroom door which had been pushed open. I immediately grabbed my baseball bat and ran to the living room wearing only my undershorts to find some ugly thug sitting on my couch with my VCR in his hands. When he saw me he ran out the front door quickly with the VCR. I think he was waiting for my wife to come out of the room first so he could try to assault her. We found out later that the Blackstone rangers street gang had infiltrated our apartment complex and were selling drugs and soliciting prostitution from any unit they could take over.

We suddenly felt unsafe in our residence. My wife moved in with her sister and I moved in with my mom and dad. My job laid me off again and I went on welfare to get food stamps in order to feed my kids.

Nobody ever said that life would be easy, in fact everybody I remember always talked about how hard life was, how you would struggle to make it day to day then you would die. I very seldom remember anyone saying that "life was fun" that they enjoyed waking up every day and taking a stroll through their beautiful neighborhood.

There were not many good jobs available to anyone without a college degree. I had passed several employment tests for career level opportunities as a proofreader and computer technician with flying colors only to be told "you don't have enough experience" or "I am not sure that you can make the transition from the warehouse to an administration position". I figured that I could get hired as a bus Driver, factory worker, security officer or an office worker and those are the jobs that I was applying for but for some reason I was not getting any job offers. I figured the employers saw my zip code and wouldn't hire me because I was from an inner-city neighborhood filled with crime and poverty. I didn't have the money to take care of my family or myself not to mention paying for college, but I was determined to get my college degree because I figured that I could never earn enough money to pay bills, buy a house, take care of a family and save for retirement unless I received a degree. I also knew that I deserved to have a college degree and my goal was to get a Bachelor's degree. I also couldn't stand staying in my mother's house again, and living back in the neighborhood I grew up in. It was déjà vu and I felt like I was going backwards over and over again.

My sister, Julia, was living in Dallas Texas with her husband Clint. They had a beautiful, cozy home in a nice neighborhood and invited me to come to Dallas, Texas and relocate. She told me that I was too smart to be unemployed and that jobs were plentiful in Dallas Texas in 1985. I had privately decided to take my sister up on the opportunity and wanted to hit the road early and make good time during the day light hours. One morning before 5am I loaded up my car with only a few clothes, my necessary belongings and took off to Dallas, Texas in my beat up red 1977 Camaro. It was about a fifteen-hour trip to Dallas, Texas and I didn't figure anyone would miss me until after I had arrived at my sisters' house. I only had about $200.00 to travel with, but gas was only $1.10 per gallon and with a perfect trip I would make the 900-mile trip to Texas spending under $100.00

There were holes in the floorboard of my Camaro that generated from the ice and salt on the heels of my female passengers' shoes in the wintertime. For six winters the heels of their shoes grinded into the rusted floorboard and continuously enlarged the holes. I had to be careful not to drop anything of value on the floor of the car because I was scared it might fall through the holes and wind up on the highway behind me. It rained and stormed for the first ten hours of my road trip and my windshield wiper would get stuck on the driver's side metal trimming every time they swayed from left to right. My door handles were broken off and I had to constantly lower my driver's side window with pliers and pull the windshield wiper with my left hand from the crack in the metal window trimming to get the windshield wiper unstuck.

The temperature was about 40 degrees outside, and my heat was not working. There was a steady rain coming down and my fingers were getting numb even though I had gloves on. West Memphis, Arkansas was about 80 miles away and it was nearing midnight. Patches of fog had begun darting across the highway. I use to ride in the front seat with my dad all the time when we traveled on the highway. On one trip we were traveling through I- 65 to Sheffield, Alabama and Dad and I were talking about baseball. My mom, brother and sister were asleep. Only dad and I were awake. While we were conversing, a thick fog began to drift across the highway and then all of a sudden it was totally dark. Dad slowed the car down and veered to the right where we noticed several cars pulled up on the shoulder. There were cars piled up on the other side of the highway. Right in front of us was the toll booth. The other drivers had not seen the tool booth due to the intense fog. Dad eased the car on through the toll booth and we proceeded on our trip without any further incident. My mom, brother and sister were still asleep and never knew what happened.

My mind also wandered back to the time I had driven this same Camaro with Chuck and Rodney downstate to Carbondale Illinois. We rode the riverboats with some pretty girls, played basketball with some of my old college friends, and had a few beers. When darkness came, we left Carbondale totally exhausted, and I drove through a foggy rainstorm for four hours in the middle of the night. I remember that I kept falling asleep and Rodney or Chuck would grab the steering wheel until I regained my composure. We were only 100 miles from home, and I fell asleep again. Rodney grabbed the wheel and told me to wake up but my eyes would not open. They were shut tight. I rightfully panicked and turned the wheel to the right and rode off the shoulder into a ditch and smashed the radiator into a fence. It's funny how driving on the highway gives you time to remember things you had forgotten about. My back was tired, and I was getting hungry. I decided to stop at a motel in West Memphis, Arkansas to get some food, a cold beer and some sleep. I left the motel at about 6 am the next morning and after about 1 hour of driving I had a flat on Interstate 40 west in Lonoke, Arkansas. I was in such a hurry to get away from Chicago that I didn't think about checking my spare tire before I left, and I did not have a spare tire. I pushed my car backwards one mile back and up the entrance ramp and rolled it into the Shell gas station on a flat tire. There were a bunch of red necks in the gas station staring at me and looking at me like "what the hell are you doing here"? I started jacking my car up and the polyethylene bumper broke causing my car to fall to the ground. I asked the rednecks if any of them had a hydraulic jack in their pickup trucks that I could use and they looked at me like I was crazy.

Just then a muddy pickup truck drives up in the gas station. This tall skinny guy with hair all over his face drives jumps out of the vehicle. He comes right up to me and blew his unfiltered camel cigarette smoke directly in my face, and with a strong hillbilly accent said; "there's a tire shop across the highway down the hill on the road over there". I had looked across the road and I wondered why I hadn't seen it before. It seemed like the tire shop had been placed there just for me. I thanked him for the information and pushed my car across the road, down the hill and around the corner to the tire shop.

The tire attendant was surprisingly nice. He jacked up my car, looked at my tire then took it off the wheel and placed it in the water to find the leak. He looked up at me and with his cigarette still in his mouth said that "all I needed was to replace the valve on my tire" and he replaced the valve for $5.00. I was sure it would have cost more than $5.00 to fix my flat and I would have been stuck in Lonoke, Arkansas until I could get my dad to wire some funds to me. After spending $40.00 dollars on the motel and $15.00 eating, and of course the six pack. I had just a little more money than I needed for gas the rest of the way. I had lost two hours' time, but I was back on my journey to Dallas, Texas.

I had been rolling well in my Chevy for about 100 miles, when my oil started smoking. Smoke was steaming from the hood of the car, and I thought my engine was going to burn up. I pulled up into a gas station restaurant, opened up the hood and watched the smoke fly in the air. Just then a somewhat tall Caucasian man with a full beard and long hair center parted to the side walked up to my car and looked at the smoke. He courteously said "the oil is just burning off it will be fine. Where are you headed"? I told him. Dallas, Texas "You should make it", he said. Then I asked him what city I was in. He said "Texarkana." I had never heard of Texarkana, and I thought I must have been in the twilight zone because this guy looked like every white picture of Jesus that I had ever seen. I had 287 miles to go to reach my sister's house and no more money at all except $10.00 for gas to make it the rest of the way. I put my last $10.00 in the car which filled it up for the last time. I finally made it to my sister's house but not before getting lost and getting instruction from a Dallas Police officer who pulled me over for having out of state plates. Julia and Clint (my brother- in-law) greeted me with open arms and made me comfortable. They wanted me to relax, take my time and get a good job and save some money and then move into my apartment. Within two weeks, I had a good job and in one month I moved out of Julia's house and into my own apartment. I was broke but my beat-up Camaro was still running good.

I had a job and was enrolled in college. I knew things were just beginning to get better for me. Now I had a chance to start a new life and recreate myself in a different environment. It may have been the best decision I ever made to move to Texas and get away from my family and friends. I was finding out what mattered most to me in life. There were still demons that haunted me, but I was determined more than I had ever been to succeed. I never wanted to have to get food stamps. I never wanted to live on the South side of Chicago amidst the gangs in the inner city again. I had thoughts of returning to Chicago to be around family, friends and familiar surroundings but there were things that I needed to accomplish in Texas, and I was not going back. Whatever it took I was going to be successful.

Meet Your Imagination
Fulfill your fantasies.
Whatever you desire
Can be your destiny.

Believe in your dreams
And they will come true.
Build yourself a world
Tailored to fit you.

But you have to be positive
And give the best that you can give.
Be positive
Because you've got your life to live.

Life has ups and downs;
The world keeps turning round.
You've got to look up
When the sun goes down.

You've got to have strength,
Keep your head off the ground.
No matter what happens
In this life you live,
Always have faith and
Be positive.

Journey to Success

It has been nearly twenty-five years ago since March 1985 when I arrived in Texas driving in my beat up Camaro. We now have a global economy and technology has increased immensely. ATM machines, cell phones, and Viagra have been invented. In 1988 I received my Associates degree in Administrative Management from East field College in Mesquite, TX and in 1995 received my Bachelors, degree in Sociology from the University Of Texas at Dallas. Between 1990 and 1997 I worked as a Police Officer in Dallas, Texas and Richardson, Texas. My two sons are now grown, and Pam and I have divorced. We realized that we are better friends than husband and wife. Gas is now over $3.00 per gallon and the unemployment rate is higher than it has ever been in my lifetime. For the last ten years I have been employed in the mortgage industry and I live in Richardson, Texas. We elected the first Black President in 2008 as the 44th president of the United States of America, and sadly, my mom didn't live to see him get elected.

Donald J. Trump was recently elected to be the 47th president of the United States of America.

Wouldn't it be great if every day of our life went exactly the way we wanted it to go? You could get the girl, (or guy,) of your dreams, have the job or career you desire and even determine how long you live but you can't resign from life just because your position is unfavorable! (Choices, decisions, action, reaction and faith will help you succeed or fail. The way we react to situations in our life will determine our level of success.) With success comes adversity but goals can still be accomplished in spite of adversity. The way that you handle your adversity determines whether you accomplish your goals or not. Every adversity has within it the seed of a greater or equivalent benefit.

Always see adversity as a steppingstone to success". Some situations are adverse, but they can be overcome because, for every situation there is an appropriate action or reaction. If you are success-driven, then you want to make the correct move or the best choices in your life. It's not always easy but hopefully we have learned something from our past mistakes. Always visualize your success. See it. Feel it. Taste it. Imagine what you will do when you have reached your destination. Righteousness is mandatory if you want to accomplish success. The opposite brings unneeded negativity and ill fate.

You will never know all the details of how you will reach your destination but as you get closer to your success and begin to fine tune your focus, the details and road map become clearer. (The goals we set, way we react to situations in our life, and the choices we make all have a lot do to with where we are now and where we will be.)

This is the God–given power inside of us. This is where we determine our destiny. If you have not set any goals, then you cannot be successful. Success comes when your goals have been accomplished. You may be lucky if you hit the lottery or win big while gambling, but don't plan on it. That is why gambling can be a tough occupation. Fame and money do not make you successful. A famous author wrote: "the idea that acquisitions will make you happy is a big letdown for most. Eventually, the coarse, plastic, electronic nature of modern living destroys our sensitivity, and with it goes much of our real perception of life. What is important is that we learn the lessons from the mistakes we make in our life and become better individuals. Many of us come from poverty or an uneducated family where success is not the norm, and the individual has to learn or be taught to react positively in adverse situations. When the opposite happens, it is detrimental? For example: look at crime in the inner city. When I was 18, some of my friends were burglarizing houses. I could have gone with them but that wasn't my thing. I was riding in the car with my friends once when they suddenly decided to burglarize someone they knew. The guy was at home and things got a little crazy. I let my home boys know that the next time they were going to do a burglary I would be chilling out at home practicing my bass or writing songs or doing something else. In the future whenever they would ask me if I wanted to come with them to break into someone's house, I would say no, that I was busy. One time my neighbor's house was burglarized, and my dad told me that someone asked if I was involved with the burglary or if I knew who did it. I assured him that I had no part in it and the people who robbed my neighbor's house didn't talk to me about it anyway because they knew I wouldn't have participated. When you are unemployed and have a lack of finances it is important not to fall into the crime trap. Some people never find their way out of that dilemma. A few of my childhood associates or friends had served serious time in the penitentiary for assault, burglary, drugs or whatever. In 1985 the crack cocaine epidemic hit the country. It hit the South Side of Chicago bad; many people started using crack out of hopelessness. This made their condition even more hopeless. It was happening all around me and I didn't want to be a part of it. Mom asked me later if I thought that I would have gotten hooked on crack if I had stayed in that environment. I smiled and said "no". The crack epidemic played a big part in my decision to relocate.

Women were walking around skinny, looking like zombies and offering sex acts for $5.00. Most of my friends and everybody else's friends were using or selling crack. Gangs were infiltrating the neighborhoods. Crackheads and prostitutes were everywhere. My choice was to get out of the inner city of Chicago and away from the crime and violence.

What is success and how do we obtain it? How do you accomplish goals when you are economically dysfunctional and do not have any goals in life? Can you be successful and poor simultaneously?

When these questions are answered then success is easily obtainable!

How we as individuals go about achieving our personal happiness and living our lives is our **"Journey to Success"**. I have a theory that I call **"The Fallacy of Existence"**. This is where we don't think we can achieve our desired goals in life. So, we rationalize and give up on them and live just to exist. We think that because our parents are poor, and we were born without a lot of money that we will always be that way that we have come as far as we can go. Sometimes we stop trying to better ourselves because we have convinced ourselves that it is impossible to succeed. We continue to fail because we expect to fail!

On one visit to my Godfather, I sat down in his comfortable recliner while he veered into his large 300 - gallon tropical fish tank and watched his beautiful multicolored fish swim. He began orating to me about excellence and began repeating to me over and over again

"Fred J must excel", "Fred J must excel", "Fred J must excel", "Fred J must excel, let nothing discourage you in your quest to excel!!"

"At that time, I did not have the faintest idea of what my God father was talking about but he was a smart and much respected man, so I knew he was trying to tell me something. Now I know. "A person should realize that the major disappointment in life is not failing to reach your goals, but not having any goals to reach.

No one wants to die without fulfilling their dreams but one must dream or they will die.

It is not a calamity to be unable to capture your dreams and goals.

But it is a disaster to not have any goals or dreams to capture.

It is not a disgrace to not excel

But it is a disgrace to not try to excel"

Between stimulus and response there is a space.

In that space lays our freedom and power to choose our response.

In these choices lie our growth and happiness.

There should always be something important that we look forward to doing each day that makes us happy. Goals must be specific, measurable, obtainable, relevant, time oriented as well as righteous if you expect to ever have peace of mind.

We all resist change, but change is inevitable in life, especially if we hope to succeed at anything. If you want to succeed in life, you have to make good choices, set challenging goals and react positively to all situations, even if they are adverse or negative. In some environments it is extremely difficult to react positively to our circumstances. Neighborhood distractions such as gang violence can keep you from accomplishing your objectives unless they are eliminated from your life. For instance, a young person growing up in a low income, high crime neighborhood would obviously want to overcome this adverse situation in their life and earn at least an average income and live in a relatively peaceful crime free neighborhood. Unfortunately, a good job and a nice home in a pleasant community do not happen by just wanting it. There are steps that need to be taken to acquire success.

A minor living under adverse or dysfunctional conditions would need assistance (from an outsource source) in order to get out of their negative environment. Young men who have been in trouble with the law have a tough time getting a job and making adequate wages when they are not in jail and usually wind up hustling to get money. Even this situation can be overcome with change.

Mistakes are a big part of life, and I make plenty of them way too often. Even after I knew the direction I was supposed to be going I allowed myself to be distracted from my goals. If you are in the middle of a competitive chess game and accidentally touch your queen, then you still have to move the queen and may end up losing it. End of Game! You can't take back your move. When I think back to all the mistakes that I have made in life I wish that I could take them back. I would never have gotten caught up with the gangs and dropped out of school at fifteen years of age. I would have completed high school and went to straight to college and pursued my master's degree and become gainfully employed in the career of my choice before I was married.

At that time, I didn't understand that Black males and Black women in the inner city were victims of racial discrimination, racial isolation, and experienced a concentrated disadvantage. I did not understand that over 30% of black males without a high school education wind up being incarcerated in state or federal prisons. The mistakes go on and on and I can't take them back. You can't take yours back either, but I have learned to never touch my queen before I know where I am going to move it.

You will not be in the same position you are in now for the rest of your life.

Your situation will get better or worse depending on your reaction to daily challenges.

There have been periods in my life when I wasted so much time, watching the game with the fellows or "just chilling". Socializing is fine and it can be fun, but time goes by quickly. I had to ask myself do I really deserve to socialize so much while accomplishing so little. Every day brings forth the opportunity to continue working towards your objective. Success and happiness do not depend on money.

Many people fall into the trap that money is success and turn to criminal activity for income. There are people who have gained financial success and made bad mistakes, or unrighteous choices and squandered their fortune quicker than they made it and lived in poverty.

I have done foolish things in order to obtain money, selling weed when I was fifteen, selling other people's books in college, gambling, running up credit card debt etc.

My Dad is a very successful man, yet he was never wealthy. He didn't have a college education, but he worked hard, saved a little money and encouraged his children to get an education. At this moment he is 82 years old and in good health. Hopefully, we have all had some success in our lives. The "feeling of success" can keep you focused on your goals in tough times. Remember that feeling of success when things get difficult.

"Desire and belief, backed by faith and a willingness to do whatever it takes will always bring success". Fame and Money do not make you successful and money is not the true measure of a man or woman. When monetary success is achieved the choices and decisions in life are more difficult. Many famous people have made millions of dollars and lost it all or went to jail due to bad decisions. That is not success. There may be periods when we lose confidence and become fragmented as a person. Life may wear you down sometimes. Every day brings forth the opportunity to overcome any negative circumstances that were previously in your life. I thank God every morning for another opportunity to do well.

When we recognize this pattern in our behavior we need to "fix ourselves and we must refuse to quit and focus on where we are going instead of the problem we are currently experiencing

John played guitar like Jimmie Hendrix and tried to live like him as well. We had been writing songs and playing music together since the eighth grade. By the time we were twenty, John had run afoul of the law and had done some time in jail. I bought a hot colored television set from him and nearly went to jail for pawning it. The cops came by the house and told mom that the TV came from a burglary done on Thanksgiving Day while a family was eating dinner, and they needed me to come to the station to be identified. Dad took me to the station and the lady said that I was not one of the burglars.

We continued to write songs and jam together, but John was still participating in illegal activity. He was on probation and didn't want to go back to jail but he couldn't change his reaction when his crime partners would ask him if he was in on the next burglary. John wound up doing more criminal activity and eventually was incarcerated for several years. John's whole life changed negatively after that because of his bad choices. I loved my friends even though most of them were either thugs or musicians who smoked too much weed. But I couldn't change them, and I thought they were the only people that cared about me. It was hard to get jobs when you lived in the inner city, and I certainly did not want to raise my family in that environment. I didn't want to fail to thrive: live in a high crime and drug area, be unemployed and not contribute positively to society.

When I was married and working a full-time job and going to college in Texas, I didn't have time for myself, friends, or family for that matter. I partially blamed my wife and kids for my lack of success, and I wished that I had gone to college and obtained my Bachelor's and Master's degree right out of high school then gotten married later instead of the other way around. I realize now that it was my responsibility to prepare myself financially prior to getting married. I would have been making a decent salary at a relatively young age and could have bought a home for my family and would not have had to go to school and work while raising a family.

I did not receive my associates degree until I was thirty-one and my Bachelor's degree until I was thirty five years old. I realized later that it is up to each individual to seize the moment in life. If you do not succeed in reaching your destination you cannot blame other people for your failure to succeed.

Recently I spoke with Karen, who is an old friend of mine that I have known since the third grade. I had not spoken to her in twenty-five years. She had still been in touch with some of our old friends and she looked me up to see how I was doing. She called and asked me "How is your life, are you happy"? I somewhat suspiciously responded, "Yes, I am happy. Why do you ask?", "everybody I speak to is so unhappy with their life, I am surprised, you are the first person I have heard say they were happy in a long time." She gave me several reasons why these people were not happy. Some of the examples were: poverty, bad health, joblessness, loneliness, unhappiness, and on and on. Love, peace, and happiness are all states of the mind and money can't buy them. We all need something that we love in our life, a meaning to live and a reason to be happy each day. We must find it and hold on to it and never let anyone take it away. Success and happiness are intertwined.

> I started wondering what my life meant to me.
>
> Was I meant to struggle or was I meant to be free
>
> Am I stuck in a vacuum?
>
> Or is it my destiny to be happy
>
> Like a bird, and fly high into the sky?

That is when I began my Journey to Success.

Relationships

There are many different types of relationships: business, friends, relatives, sexual, social, student, teacher, working, etc. Some of these people do not care if you fail or succeed. Even in personal relationships your partner may not support you in the pursuit of your goals. What do you do when your friends and associates don't believe or care if you accomplish your goals? Every relationship has a contract and, in my opinion, if your goals are more important than the relationship, then you should end the relationship, however, as you may know it is not always easy to end an unwanted relationship.

When I was living on the south side of Chicago people were unemployed and dying from gang violence on a daily basis and no one in the city government seemed to care. Most of the south side citizens were democratic and didn't trust the republicans in the city government. Factory jobs that our moms and dads worked at for years and raised their families on had been moved to the suburbs and most parents could no longer afford to send their children to college. Most of my associates tried to stay away from the streets by going to school or working, but the streets will get you if you have too much time on your hands. The streets have beaten a lot of us down. Beat us down to the ground. You lived or you died in the streets. It was just a way of life in the hood. Other than the streets what else did a poor black man own?

When I was twenty-two years old, I was being pulled in so many different directions by so many different people. I didn't know who I was or what I was capable of achieving. I needed a new beginning, a different geographical area. I needed to get away from the things that were tuning

29

me down. When I moved from the inner city of Chicago to Texas and into a racially diverse area, I developed new relationships and changed my behavior to fit my new environment. Your home neighborhood plays a big factor in your success. People that you have known for years may not want you to grow as a person or move on in your life because you will leave them behind. I loved my friends in Chicago dearly because we grew up together and went through most of the same adversities. When I made the decision to relocate my friends wished me well, but I sensed they generally thought I would fail in my relocation attempt and wind up back on the south side of Chicago.

After I had lived in Texas for a while, the way I lived my life and the type of people I associated with had changed. I completed my BA in Sociology and had become a police officer and was cultivating relationships with people that were going in the direction of my choice. I began to realize that every relationship in my life was important.

I have learned immensely from them. The relationships you are in may determine whether you succeed or fail. Some of the relationships I have known have been quite interesting.

Suzette was a beautiful, intelligent, and seductive lady. She was a 5ft' 8" light skinned African American woman with a very curvy figure. Marvin, her husband, was athletically built, very dark and about 6ft' 2". Marvin insisted that Suzette stay home with their three children instead of working. Sometimes Marvin worked two jobs to provide financial support for the family. After twenty plus years of marriage Suzette started having a relationship with another man. She started drinking and using drugs. She had never done drugs before in their relationship. Their marriage broke up.

Both these people were friends of mine. But the point is people "change" and if you are in a relationship their change affects you. You have to decide how to react to the change. Your reaction will determine if the relationship continues to positively exist.

In this case it did not. Their marriage broke up and they went their separate way.

My friend's son Kevin was an eighteen-year-old high school football star. I used to coach basketball against Kevin when he was in middle school. He ran a 4-3 forty, but he tore his MCL in the high school playoffs. Several colleges were recruiting him, but they were no longer interested in giving him a scholarship after the injury. Kevin started hanging out in the streets with hustlers and drug dealers and never finished high school. He started dealing and using drugs. Eventually he was caught by the cops with drugs on his possession and had to do time in jail. When Kevin was released after two years, he started right back dealing and using drugs and hanging out on the streets.

My old friend Emanuel loved to party. He would get paid, and we would go clubbing and he bought all the drinks for his partners. The drinks were always on him. Later I found out that Emanuel was in debt with his car note, mortgage, payday loans and other debts. He also had a cocaine habit no one knew about until later. I don't have any idea of what has happened to him. I do remember that I was given a promotion at work, and I couldn't hang out and party with Emanuel during the week anymore. So, I stopped hanging out with him and it pissed him off. We haven't talked since then, but I heard he went through a tough time for a while with drugs and his health.

The family relationship is one of the most serious relationships you will ever have.

The way you react in your family relationship tends to stay with a person and the family their whole life. Even after we are grown some of us hide our beliefs and principles for the sake of peace with family, or friends. Relationship choices have to be made over and over again.

Do your families, friends or coworkers determine your success?

Marriage is an extremely interesting relationship. Your relationship must be in harmony with the goals you expect to achieve if you expect to succeed at anything. If you are a preacher, would you want to be married to a stripper? Could a school teacher have a successful relationship with a traveling musician? Relationships are developed for many reasons, however, a person's body, mind and spirit as well as their goals, should be carefully examined before entering into matrimony. What do you plan to accomplish together and how do you plan to achieve it? A relationship based solely on sex is purely physical and short term at most. Contrary to popular opinion, it is my belief that money or sex is not a legitimate reason to get married.

My friend Robert has been married to Yolanda for ten years and has two children. He has an eight-year-old son and a ten-year-old daughter. He has sex with different women on a consistent basis in spite of being married. He spends his money loosely on women and likes to have a good time partying at the club. He told his girlfriend Martha that his wife doesn't like sex. Maratha has bipolar disorder; she said that Robert takes advantage of her medical condition and uses her sexually and that Robert doesn't care about her medical condition or his wife.

When I was in my very early twenties my "home boys" and I would challenge each other to see who could get the most girlfriends at one time. We would try to have different ladies all the time with no commitment or serious relationship. It was fun but it was also dangerous.

Tyrone was a smooth operator. He was athletic, tall and the ladies thought he was good looking. He slept with his "friends" women if he could get away with it and he didn't care if they knew about it. He was always sleeping with several women at the same time. He told all his ladies upfront that he would have other girlfriends. Well one day Tiffany came over his house while he was having sex with Lisa. Tiffany knew that Tyrone was home, and she waited for him to come out of the front door, and she stabbed him in the chest with a screwdriver. Tyrone now has some permanent scars on his chest and not many friends because no one can trust him. I know I don't talk to him anymore.

Erick was hooked on cocaine and used to have sex with different women. He would beat his steady girlfriend up badly all the time Eric was a good friend of mine, but he was mean to his girlfriends. One day Eric's sister called me and told me that Eric's girlfriend had stabbed him to death after he beat her one day.

Chester is Black and he lives with Cassandra who is white. They are both in their mid-forties and have grown children.

Chester's family doesn't want him to be with a white woman and they have told him this. Cassandra's family is racist, but they have accepted the relationship even though they have family functions without inviting Cassandra and Chester. Chester and Cassandra both enjoy their relationship but are careful not to step on either family's toes. The in-laws don't know each other and never communicate due to bigotry, hatred and racism. (Whose footsteps are you trying to keep up with?)

Kill Racism

Before racism kills you and me,
That's not the way society is supposed to
be.
We need to live in unity.

Hatred
Between the colors of the skin
Makes it impossible for us to blend
And create a world where we transcend.

Bigotry
Practiced in the past
Can no longer last.
We must eliminate it fast!

Kill racism
Before racism kills you and me.

No one should live in poverty
While others live in luxury.

Equality,
Justice in the legal system
Needs to be corrected.
We all should be protected
In the land of the free.

Kill racism before
Racism kills you and me.

Sex

My hands massaged her nipples, gently pulling on them with my fingers while caressing her perfect mounds with the palm of my hands. Her beautiful, sculpted breast demanded my attention as our bodies lay together while her soft hands were stroking me gently.

One evening about thirty years ago, my dad asked me if I was having sexual relations. I was shocked that he would even ask me that question. What nearly twenty-year-old man is not having or at least trying to have sex? He told me there were some prophylactics under his mattress and then raised the mattress to show where they were carefully hidden in the center.

Dad advised me not to have sex without them due to the risk of contracting a sexually transmitted disease. He also advised that if I didn't use them, I may become a father before I had become a man. I remember looking at him like he had lost his mind. I wasn't going to talk to dad about my sex life and I didn't want to use his rubbers. They didn't fit well. They were tight and pulled on the hairs around my genitals. It also took time to put them on, which delayed the sex act and sometimes caused me to lose my erection and that meant "no sex". Anyway, I told dad "Ok, I will, use the Trojans if I needed to. A week later dad called me in his room and asked me "What happened to all the Trojans?"

During this period of my life, I was lucky to have not caught a disease or become a father too early. The Trojans were all gone but I hadn't used them having sex. I wasted them trying them on for comfort and size. I tried to use them, but I could never get used to them.

Discussing sex with your children is a cumbersome task and can be uncomfortable but it must be done. You can't rely on schools to teach education to your children. If parents don't discuss sex with their children, they may receive their sexual education from an irresponsible source. My sons are eighteen months apart and when it was time for me to discuss sex with my two sons, I didn't do any better than my dad. I may have been worse than dad. They were about seventeen or eighteen years old and had begun bringing their girlfriends home and I felt like it was time to discuss sexual relations with them. I asked them "Is there anything you need to know about sex"? They looked at me just like I had looked at my dad and then began laughing. I told them to always treat girls like a lady, and if they needed any sexual information that I was available, and then I left the room feeling like I had not accomplished my mission.

It would be nice to think that one evening our parents decided to go on a romantic date shopping at the mall, then to dinner at a nice restaurant, after that dancing at the club with a hot band, maybe a few drinks then came home and made passionate love to achieve conception. However, in reality that is probably not the case.

I had my first girlfriend when I was in the third grade. I remember that we liked each other but I didn't understand why. Neither of us knew anything about relationships or sex. What could two eight-year-old children see in each other? Even back in the third-grade boys would try to beat you up if a girl liked you and they wanted her to like them. I had several fights with guys in school over pretty girls.

When I was in the seventh grade, my girlfriend invited me to come over during lunch time. I don't think that grade school kids can leave the campus at lunch time now but "back in those days" we got into all kinds of mischief at lunch time. Her mom was at work and her dad was nonexistent. We grinded, kissed, touched each other in private places and got ourselves all worked up unnecessarily instead of having lunch. On the way back to school I couldn't walk without doubling over and I had to hold my stomach.

I remember that afternoon in class my stomach hurt, and I began to cramp. One of my older friends told me that I had "blue balls" and next time to make sure I got my "rocks off". I didn't like the feeling that blue balls gave me, so it was a while before I messed with girls again.

When I was a freshman in high school my girlfriend and I got involved in some heavy kissing, grinding and petting. I was all worked up and I remembered the advice that my friend had given me. My girlfriend told me she was not allowed to have sexual relations, and we were not going all the way, so we grinded and grinded until I finally released myself in my pants. I remember covering it up with my hands trying to hide it from her mom as I left the house that evening. I am certain that her mom knew what was going on. But I had figured out how not to catch a case of the blue balls.

My girlfriend and I were both sixteen years old when we lost our virginity. Neither one of us understood what sex was all about. We certainly did not know what love meant. She didn't want to go all the way but thought I would want another girlfriend if she didn't perform sexually, and I didn't feel like I was a man until I had sex. When the sex was over

I didn't feel very satisfied and neither did my girlfriend.

Sex is the most beautiful act in the world when two people mutually desire to please each other. The pleasure of being pleased sexually is immeasurable. An exciting, stimulating sex life can increase your happiness by decreasing your anxiety and stress; however, there are barriers to sexual enjoyment. Irresponsible sexual behavior can lead to sexual abuse or sex addiction, which can ruin your potential to be successful in this life. Many men think that since women are physically inferior to men that women are the weaker sex and consequently men often try to use women as sex toys through coercion, power manipulation or violence. More men are deeming it acceptable behavior to cheat on their wives and activity at adult clubs has become more promiscuous. Aggressive sexual behavior towards any women is unwarranted regardless of the situation and should never be exhibited Sexism in any form should not be tolerated and is unacceptable, immoral behavior.

I wish I could take back the day that I pressured my girlfriend to have sex with me. In retrospect I would have waited until I understood what love and sex really meant, until I understood the importance of sharing love together.

When I Saw You for the First Time

I knew you were meant for me.

I have always wanted a girl like you,

Because you are my Dream Lady!

You are my Dream Lady!

You are a picture of delight,

Sitting on satin sheets under rose-colored

lights.

Your tender brown skin all dressed in white,

You're smiling with all your might,

You and me in the night! Dream Lady!

You are my Dream Lady!

We can really live our lives together;

You are more beautiful than you were

In my dreams.

We can be friends and lovers, actually—

Sometimes dreams mean more than they seem.

Dream Lady!

Was that you inside of my dream?

Dream Lady!

Health and Athleticism

As a child I loved sports and all athletics, but baseball was my favorite game. If I wasn't playing baseball, I was probably reading a book about it. I'll never forget when I was nine years old, and I tried out for the little league baseball team. The coach hit the ball deep in the outfield and while I was running to catch up to it, I tripped over a large brick and fell down. But I knew that I had to catch that ball. I got up and ran it down, caught it with my back to the fence and then threw the baseball to the coach. I could catch and pitch as well as anyone my age and better than most people that were older than me. There is no doubt in my mind that I would have been a successful professional baseball player had I continued to play the game past high school and into college. Basketball was fun and my play brother, Ted, used to take me to school on the court when I was a teenager. Ted was a few years older than me and physically superior at that time. I tried to get him on the basketball court a few years ago for a rematch but Ted wanted to stay undefeated. Football was not my game at all. I could catch the ball, but I was not big or very fast. I had broken both of my legs as a youth, but I still wanted to play football when I first went to high school, but mom wouldn't let me play because both of my legs had been broken. Mom told me that when I was two years old a fat three-year-old boy was chasing me in church and he caught me and fell on me and my leg broke, but I don't remember any of it. When I was ten years old my brother and I were playing 'fighting' in the basement, and he fell on my leg, and it bent under me in an awkward way and fractured in two or three places. I remember walking slowly to school in the winter snow, and up and down the stairways with crutches for two months. My friends used to call me crip back then. Sometimes they would grab my crutches and run with them. Mom didn't believe in missing school and a broken leg was certainly no excuse.

My brother and I and some friends began studying martial arts when we were twelve or thirteen years old. We studied Kung Fu, Tai chi, Aikido, Judo and anything else we could to learn to defend ourselves in the tough streets of Chicago's South Side. A few of my friends and I went to "Big Buddies Youth Center" to study Karate, Judo, and Kung Fu with a master martial artist. The instructor made us fight with full contact all the time. I had to fight my older friends, Arthur, Daryl, and Ted. They constantly kicked my butt.

Thursdays were called "Blood Thursday" because the instructor fought all of his students at once until someone began bleeding. I will never forget the class session when Arthur, Ted, Darryl and I attacked the instructor. We had a plan. Arthur was the craziest so he would attack the instructor first, then Darryl would throw a punch. Darryl was a full back on the high school football team, and he was built like one too. He could beat anybody in the neighborhood. Ted was very good at judo, and he would go in for the flip. I would attack next. Arthur, Darryl and Ted went in for the kill. The next thing I knew the instructor leg swept Arthur to the mat threw Darryl aside and threw a punch at Ted. Luckily, he missed but half his arm went right through the wall. When we saw his fist lodged in the big hole in the wall, we immediately took off running and hid in closets or anywhere else in the building. He chased us all down and made us come back to class and then chewed our butts out for running. Daryl went home and never came back to class again. The next week the instructor didn't come to teach class because he was in the hospital. We were told that seven men jumped him, and he killed four of them and put the other three in the hospital. I remember hoping that I could defend myself as well if I were attacked. You have to be able to defend yourself in the hood. My first real test to see if I could defend myself came one summer when I was fourteen years old. My cousin Roslyn came to spend the summer with us. Roslyn was very pretty, and she was the same age as my sister. The bad guys from around the corner came around and started harassing Julia and Roslyn. I knew one of them well, Andre, who was a year older than me and thought he could whip me. He and his older brothers were thugs. Roslyn gets into a fist fight with him, and he hits her in the chest. I couldn't believe that he hit a lady and especially my cousin. Without thinking I immediately jumped in his face and confronted him. He threw a few punches at me, and I blocked them, danced a little and then knocked him out with a right cross to the chin. He was lying right there in the street on the side of my mom's house. I was stunned but I wasn't scared to fight anybody anymore. When I was fifteen years old, I began jogging 5 miles daily. I stopped eating red meat and pork and I weighed a meager 135 pounds. My brother, good friend Jamal and I studied Tai Chi with Hakeem who was an orthodox Muslim. He was a tall bearded graceful man that seemed to know everything about the universe. He taught us life knowledge, martial arts and philosophy. He even played a little saxophone and sometimes we would have improvisational jazz jam sessions. I studied Tai Chi until I was twenty years old. I believe I was equivalent to a brown belt and my brother later received his black belt in Aikido.

When I was twenty years old, I went to the Air Force and ate all the potatoes I could eat to gain weight. I accelerated my weight up to a whopping 150 lbs. I stayed around 150 lbs. until I was thirty years old then fattened up to about 160 lbs. At 5' 10 ½" tall I probably should have weighed more but weight training was not popular then and I was unable to afford it anyway. When I reached thirty years old, I wanted to be a Police officer, and I needed to get my weight up to 175 lbs. and add definition and muscle to my frame. I began body building and eating three good meals a day and it took me about one year to raise my weight to 175lbs. Gradually I increased my strength to where I could bench press my weight. By the time I was thirty-two years old, I weighed 185 lbs. and could bench press 205 lbs. easily but I couldn't fit my old pants and needed a new wardrobe. Eventually I realized that my ideal weight was 174 to 182 lbs.

In August 2002, I was hospitalized with deep vein thrombosis and spent two weeks in the hospital. I wasn't sure that I was going to make it out of there alive. The doctor came into my room to discuss my condition with me, and I had a ridiculous since of humor, I asked him, "Doc what is the worst thing that could happen to me right now"?

He said "you have active clots in your deep veins, and we are trying to prevent them from going to your heart and causing a pulmonary embolism. If the clots burst before they can be thinned out, your left leg will have to be severed to stop the clots from traveling upwards to your heart and lung". I quickly shut up and lay back down. The Chaplin came in next to pray for me and he also left a last will and testament for me to complete. After he left, I did more praying than I have ever done in my life. I promised God that if he brought me out of the hospital that I would live my life right. My left leg had swollen up 4 inches larger than my right leg and there was insufficient blood flow from my foot to my knee. They continuously brought me food that I didn't eat, like white bread, French toast and pancakes. One morning after about eight days, I was tired of eating breakfast that I did not like and not having taken a shower. I got out of bed and threw my sheets to the floor and went to the lobby and insisted that my sheets be changed. I also demanded them to get my breakfast and dinner selection corrected. I then went and took a long overdue shower. Later in the day, my cousin Karla, who is a retired head nurse called to check on me and I proudly told her what I had done. Surprising to me she sternly told me to stay in the bed like the doctor told me, and don't get up until they say that I can. Karla said that I was lucky that the nurse didn't find me lying on the floor.

For two more weeks I would lay in bed looking out the window and watching all the people come and go. I wondered where everyone was going and why none of my friends had visited me. I didn't think that I would ever get released from the hospital. It took about three weeks before the doctors could get my blood thinned out enough to stop the clotting and I could finally get up out of the bed. (The doctor said that I could be released from the hospital but that I might never be able to run 5 miles like I was used to running before.) He also said that I had an abnormal hereditary blood disorder and there was no guarantee that I would not have another episode of DVT. The possibility existed that it could be life threatening. He said that I may have to take Coumadin for the rest of my life. I was overjoyed to be leaving the hospital, but I cried enough tears to create my own river. The diagnosis nearly scared me into never working out again but not quite. When I was released from the hospital my leg was swollen and I was taking heavy doses of Coumadin and pain killers. I continued to train in spite of the pain. I prayed over and over again to get my health back. I met a great Doctor in Garland Texas, who told me if I kept my stress level to a minimum and my heart rate normal that he could take me off of the Coumadin. After one year of dieting and steady conditioning all of my blood levels were normal, and Doctor Li was able to remove me from all medication. Since I had been on leave of absence from work, I didn't get a paycheck from work until three weeks after I was released from the hospital. It seemed like I could never get caught up on my bills and my rent eventually went two months behind. I was always getting eviction notices. My wife and I had recently separated, and I was taking the bus to work because I could not afford a car and to make matters worse the Internal Revenue Service began garnishing half of my paycheck for back taxes that I had owed since 1985. I was ready to throw the towel in on my life but after reflecting on my past actions and reactions, I understood why I had reached this uneventful period in my life. I realized that it was time to change my negative reactions to the adversity I had been experiencing. I began to make positive choices and eliminate negative people and situations from my life. I took on more responsibility at work and was soon promoted to management. In one month, I went from being 2 months behind in my rent to moving into a new apartment. I saved some money and contacted a certified public accountant and had the garnishments by the IRS stopped. Why had I not always reacted positively to negative circumstances in my life before? Well seven years later I was in nearly perfect shape, running 3 to 5 miles and bench pressing 205lbs. My weight was comfortable at 178 lbs., and I was no longer taking any medication at all. Most people have worked out at some point in their lives but for various reasons some of us became unmotivated and got out of the habit of exercising.

Then you go to the doctor, and he (or she) tells you that your cholesterol or blood pressure is too high or too low and you are twenty or more pounds overweight. Of course, your diet has a lot to do with your health. If you eat healthy you will visit the doctor less than if you are eating unhealthily. It can be debatable on what foods not to eat or avoid, but ultimately you have to decide what is best for your body. The point is: If you have the desire to be healthy and in shape you can do it. Just put your mind and your body to it. Working or studying long hours will take a toll on your body. Heavy schedules will fatigue you and stress you out if your heart is not getting enough cardiovascular exercise. You can be the most successful person that ever lived but if you are unhealthy, you probably won't be happy regardless of your fame or money. Everyone needs to exercise daily. Your mind needs rest and time to process information in order to properly function. It has been said that "your body is your temple". Do you want to destroy your own "temple" or enhance its beauty? It is your choice! Good health and success go together.

Move Your Body

Slide and groove across the floor,
Work your body.
Bring it back and go some more,
Move your body.

Make your muscles tear, then grow,
Push your body.
Stretch those legs and bend real low.

Everybody needs to exercise
To pump the heart and make your endorphins
flow.
Train your body;
You'll want to do it more and more.

When you feel the pain
And the sweat begins to pour,
You will start to glow
And will want to
Move your body more and more.

Spirituality

My brother, sister and I were baptized at an early age and were very active in the church since as far back as I can remember. Dad was a Sunday school superintendent and mom taught Sunday school and later became a minister. We went to church in the Inglewood district of Chicago, a neighborhood known for drugs, gangs, rape, poverty, theft, violence and whatever other crime you can think of. I took the bus home from church a few times and while walking to the bus stop the neighborhood thugs would holler out things like "hey church boy you got any change?" or "let me talk to you for a minute." The bus never came fast enough for me. Every Sunday afternoon we would come home from church to the aroma of a delicious, hot fried chicken dinner and buttery mashed potatoes seasoned with Lawry's. Nobody cooked Sunday dinners quite like mom!

I have always loved listening to a good preacher and hearing a good choir sing on Sunday. One Sunday, a preacher's sermon touched my heart when he spoke about how we should be just like Jesus. I thought, what would Jesus have done when the gangs pulled knives on him and demanded him to sell drugs, or when his associates and peers asked him to help break into their neighbor's house? No one respected anyone on the south side of Chicago, and I did not respect myself. I was not the messiah; I was just another poor black man trying to pull himself up by his boots strap. If I ever expected to achieve my goals in life, I could not continue to make the same mistakes that I had made in the past. I realized that I had to change internally if I ever expected to become more like Jesus.

I remember the morning my dad caught me gazing into the universe looking at the sky and counting the stars while pondering the creation of life. Dad told me "You know that man could not have put the universe in place, why even ask if there is a creator of the universe". Does it really matter where we go after we leave earth, or if we go anywhere else at all? What does religion and spirituality have to do with the meaning of life? If you have pondered over these questions, then you are not alone.

"In the beginning God created the heavens and the earth."

"In the name of Allah, the beneficent, the merciful.

Praise be to Allah."

"Nam Myo ho rang gey kyo."

"The wisdom of philosophy ends with the physical world.

Beyond the stars it can only imagine God's essence!"

A "marriage" of love - between Yahweh and his chosen people.

Hail Mary, full of grace.

Our Lord is with you..

Amen.

I often thought about what would have happened the day I was stabbed if Chuck had not turned around in the car and come back for me. I may have been repeatedly stabbed and could have been tragically killed. After that I began studying different religions to understand the different views regarding the hereafter. I went to the Buddhist temple, the Catholics church, Islamic Mosque, Jehovah Witness places of worship. We would argue over which religion was the best and the right way. I found that all of the different religious groups sincerely belief that their religion is the only way to heaven or eternal life. My religious study was educational but why I was here on earth now and what are other galaxies of the universe here for and how do we succeedin this life and the next? These are the questions that I wanted answers to and in my opinion they had more to do with spirituality than religion. It is inevitable that one day our lives on earth will come to an end. The only question is how and when it will happen. Hopefully we will all have a long life and our transition will come from natural causes, but death could come from an accident, bad health or a sudden and unexpected tragedy. And just like your birthday, you will have very little control over when your angel arrives. Death is a part of life and the sooner we understand and realize that existence is forever after and forever on, the better we can enjoy our lives our earth.

> All over the world,
> Everybody suffers;
> Everyone shares some pain.
>
> Wherever you go,
> Life is different,
> Yet it's really just the same.
> It makes you wonder
> If this all
> Is really just a game?
>
> People die,
> But God lingers on.
> How much longer will this go on?
> In this cruel and wicked world,
>
> In this cruel and wicked world,
> People die,
> But God lingers on.
> How much longer will this go on?
> In this cruel and wicked world.

During a close chess game if you make a significant mistake, you will probably lose.

Life is not a game. Life gives you a chance to correct your mistakes before you lose. Prayer, meditation and positive affirmations place me in the state of mind that enables me to make good decisions in tough circumstances.

Every morning I'm awake, I say the Lord's Prayer and I also pray:

Thank you, Lord, for everything: my life, my joy, peace and happiness
Bless me, all my family and everyone in the world
Help us all to be righteous and successful in this life
Bless those that are homeless and hungry
Forgive me for all my past mistakes
Thank you for letting me learn from my past mistakes so that I will not repeat my errors.
On this day lord let me bring positivity to every soul that I encounter
Lord, I thank you for your blessings.
Amen.

To meditate: relax and breathe in and out to the count of ten
Let your mind flow for ten minutes
Feel the energy from the sun flow down your spine from head to toe.
Focus on how you desire your events to occur
Let peace begin with you

Positive Affirmations from an unknown author

Every evening before I sleep, I positively affirm the following:

I am now willing to receive more love than I ever thought possible. I deserve to be happy and successful in all areas of my life and I am now claiming my total success and happiness for myself.

I am meeting all the right people to further my happiness, growth and perfect self-expression.

All that I desire I deserve, and it is flowing to me now from the infinite supply of the universe.

I unconditionally give myself permission to succeed in all that I do.

I deserve to me a tremendous success and to experience the rich rewards of success in all areas of my life.

There is no disability, no circumstance or situation which I cannot transform using the power of desire and belief. Desire and belief make dreams come true.

All power lies within me, and I am harnessing that power now to bring about all the positive changes that I desire.

I accept full responsibility for everything in my life. I alone create and recreate my life with every thought I think in every moment of every day.

I am not hindered by struggle or hardship for I know that I chose those circumstances, and I have the power to change them.

I live courageously for I know the more I please myself, the more I please others.

I accept only the good and positive. I reject all negatives; they do not influence my life anymore.

The world abounds with riches from an infinite supply.

All the right ideas, people and opportunities are being delivered to me now so that I may enjoy a rich and abundant life for me.

Deep in my heart I know the answers to all questions.

I am master of my mind and body.

I am knowledge, and I create my own destiny.

All these affirmations are already at work for me to bring about all that I truly desire.

I am now positively changing my life for the better in every way!

God is love, God is peace.

God is living, God is giving.

I hope you understand,

This is our master's plan.

We can't put life in the palm of our hand.

Let us live life day by day with God,

Doing what He wants us to do—

Living our lives with the love of God

And not letting the devil intercede.

God is love, God is peace.

With God's love on our side,

Stride for stride,

As we walk life's tough ride.

You can only go the right way!

Within your heart, mind, and soul,

Let it be known that

God's love is the greatest!

God's love is the greatest!

Conclusion

When a mother brings her infant home from the hospital her responsibility is to raise her child to be the best person it can be. Parents provide discipline at an early age to ensure their child makes the correct choices. As soon as the children are old enough to eat, clean their bedroom, and do chores, it is their responsibility to do so, and it is the parent's responsibility to ensure that the child assumes and accepts this responsibility. Into the teenage years it is the responsibility of the child to complete high school to the best of their ability and to pursue higher education working towards their career goals. It is the parent's responsibility to monitor their child and provide wisdom when necessary to keep the child focused on their educational objective. Assuming that we have free will and know the difference between good and bad, then we are all responsible for the choices we make in our lives every day. We as people are very similar in many ways but as individuals, we are very different and unique. A distinct feature that binds us is how morally responsible we are as a person. If a child has not been taught to assume personal responsibility while growing up, it is far reaching that they will ever be morally responsible as an adult; however, we all fall short in the area of moral responsibility. Responsibility begins with us individually in the way we raise our children and treat our wives, family and friends. We have a moral responsibility to resist and change bigotry, crime, discrimination, drugs, homelessness, hunger, racism, sexism, and any other negative forces that are trying to demonize and destroy our existence. We have a responsibility to live right and leave a legacy that our next generation can benefit from and be proud of. It is all of our responsibility to exercise high morals, be honest, and righteous law-abiding citizens. If our families, communities and society exercised collective moral responsibility then we could eliminate the negative things that poison our society such as gangs, poverty, unemployment, sexism, and violent crime. We have blamed each other and waited on our government to fix our problems long enough. When our voices are responsibly spoken together in unison, we can generate positive changes in our communities, families and society across political aisles and beyond economic and racial prejudices. If each of us who know God reach out to each other and share the knowledge and wisdom we have acquired, then we will overcome any adversity that occurs within the vicissitudes of our life.

POEMS BY FRED J.

Earthly Blues

We are down here to learn
In a world with no hope.
This life phase is no joke.
Gaining knowledge is the way to cope;
Until then, you are remote.

Problems and trials all the while
Will teach and mold us, though we get riled.
We mustn't let them make us vile;
Observe and learn to keep a smile.

We've got to help others
To understand the importance
Of helping our brother man.

If we don't learn, it's no big thing,
But our souls will sing
Earthly blues again.

Dry Days and Crisp Nights

Dry days and crisp nights
Bend my mind, make me fight.
Fill me up with hate and spite,
Like people trying to run my life,
Telling me what ain't right.
They can all go fly a kite
And keep the hell out of my sight.

Dry days and crisp nights
May change the world from wrong to
right.

If I Can Keep My Mind

I was happy; my life was filled with friends.
Now I can't stop crying;
It feels like the end.
I'm so alone, and my world's torn apart—
All I have is this bruise on my heart.

Oh, but if I can keep my mind,
I know things will change in time.
But that might not be as easy as it seems to be,
'Cause I'm so lonely now.

My thoughts disappear;
If I should vanish,
No one would care.
Sometimes I wonder if it's all worthwhile—
Being lonely and sad yet trying to smile.

Oh, but if I can keep my mind,
I know things will change in time.
If I can keep my mind.

Day by Day

Day by day,
We go our separate ways,
Reaching for something that always changes.

We fail to see
That you and I
Must live our lives together eternally.

One more time,
We'll share a world
Where we must live
And learn to give to each other.

Mission, Mission, Mission

I'm on a mission, baby;
I won't be home for a while.
You know I'll miss your loving
And your pretty sexy smile.

The hardest part of my life
Is living it without you,
But it won't be long before
All our dreams come true.

I'm on a mission, baby—
Mission, mission, mission.
I'm on a mission, baby—
Mission, mission, mission.

When I see you, it will be
The happiest day of my life.
We'll walk hand in hand
In the park.

I'll wine you and dine you,
And we'll see the latest movie.
Then I'll take you home
And make sweet love to you.

I'm on a mission;
I won't be home for a while,
But when I see you, it will be
The happiest day of my life.

Mirror of Life

You get up in the morning,
Go and comb your hair.
In the mirror,
You just look and stare.

But you don't know what you should be looking
for;
It's not your hair or the clothes you wear.
You drive your car on the expressway,
Check both mirrors to make sure you're safe.

Life is a mirror;
What you do comes back to you.
See what's around you
In the mirror of life—
A magic mirror,
See your future and live it too.

Look in the mirror,
The mirror of life.

Keep Pushing

My old man told me a long time ago,
Don't go around talking about what you don't
know.
You've got to think before you speak, you see;
You can't make no progress
If you're stepping on your feet.

You've got to keep pushing, keep pushing,
Keep pushing straight ahead—
Never ceasing, always increasing
Until your message is said.
Until the day you're dead,
Keep pushing, keep pushing,
Keep pushing straight ahead.

Together

It feels like one hundred years we've been
apart;
The time weighs heavy on my heart.
Since you've been gone,
All my nights are long,
And my whole world's been going wrong.

Baby, hurry your love back to me;
To my world, you have the key.
We'll fulfill the dreams we've seen;
We'll be together like we used to be.

There is nothing I won't do for love—
I'm sure your love's sent from above.
I'll survive on knowing soon
We'll be together like we used to be.

Since you've been gone,
All my nights are long,
And my whole world's been going wrong.
Baby, hurry your love back to me;
To my world, you have the key.
We'll fulfill the dreams we've seen;
We'll be together like we used to be.

I'll survive on knowing soon
We'll be together like we used to be.

Spiritual Journey

My mom is with Jesus now;
She has always been with Jesus
Throughout my childhood and teenage years.
Mom always preached about her love for Jesus Christ!

Christ is her Valentine.
Mom taught me to always do the right thing:
Be respectful, work hard, and always love God.
If you lose your job—love God.
If people talk bad about you—love God.
If you are ill—love God.
Love God always!

She told me that in life,
There will be obstacles and roadblocks to success;
That is when your faith is being tested.
That is when you must truly confess your love for God.

I will truly miss my mom calling me
To discuss social events, politics,
Or to see how I am doing.
But I understand that we can't stay here on earth forever.
Mom is on a spiritual journey now;
She is with the Lord.

God bless my mom.

Song for the World

Let everybody sing their praises,
Glorifying the Most High,
Acknowledging that God is ruler of
creation.

Believe it in your heart;
Live it day by day.
I'm not talking to any specific people—
This is a song for the world,
In hopes that we survive
The battle of Armageddon.

References

Through Darkness I Saw Light by Helen Felton

The Audacity of Hope by Barack Obama

The 8th Habit by Steven Covey

The Greatest Salesman in the World by Og Mandino

Man's Search for Meaning by Victor Frankl

Grow Rich with Peace of Mind by Napoleon Hill

Sixth Sense by Stuart Wilde

Live Your Dreams by Les Brown

12 Choices by David

Cottrell God is a Verb by David Copper

The Hite Report on Male and Female Sexuality by Sherry Hite

Tao Mentoring by Al Huang & Jerry Lynch

Maximum Fitness Magazine, Spring 2007 issue

Maximum Fitness Magazine, March 2009 issue

Toxicless Diet by Paul C. Bragg